Gymnastics

SPORTS SKILLS

Paul Mason

FRANKLIN WATTS
LONDON•SYDNEY

Franklin Watts
Published in Great Britain in 2017 by
The Watts Publishing Group

Copyright © The Watts Publishing Group
2015

Credits
Series Editor: Adrian Cole
Art direction: Peter Scoulding
Series designed and created for
    Franklin Watts by Storeybooks
Designer: Rita Storey
Editor: Nicola Barber
Photography: Tudor Photography,
    Banbury (unless otherwise stated)

Every attempt has been made to clear
copyright. Should there be any inadvertent
omission please apply to the publisher for
rectification.

Dewey number 796.4'4
ISBN 978 1 4451 5245 5

Printed in China

MIX
Paper from
responsible sources
FSC® C104740
FSC
www.fsc.org

Franklin Watts
An imprint of Hachette Children's Group
Part of The Watts Publishing Group
Carmelite House
50 Victoria Embankment
London EC4Y 0DZ

An Hachette UK Company
www.hachette.co.uk

www.franklinwatts.co.uk

Note: At the time of going to press, the
statistics and profiles in this book were up
to date. However, due to some gymnasts'
active participation in the sport, it is possible
that some of these may now be out of date.

Picture credits
Lilyana Vynogradova/ Shutterstock p.6,
p.20, p.22; Sergey Golotvin/ Shutterstock p.9
left & p.23; Galina Barskaya/ Shutterstock
p.9 centre right, p.26 top and right;
Lintao Zhang/ Getty Images Sport p.15;
Featureflash/ Shutterstock p17; Dean
Mouhtaropoulos/ Getty Images Sport p.27.

Cover image: Binnur Ege Gurun/Anadolu
Agency/Getty Images
All photos posed by models.
Thanks to Dené, Mel Furey, Andy Hall,
Jessica Hall and Matt Moutos.

The Publisher would like to thank the
Wade Gymnastics Club for all their help.

Previously published by Franklin Watts
as Know Your Sport Gymnastics.

Gymnastics is a
dangerous sport, and
can cause severe injuries
such as paralysis. This book
is not a self-teaching guide.
Only ever learn gymnastics
with a qualified coach.

Contents

What is Gymnastics?

Gymnastics is a sport of leaps, spins, flips and twists. It uses a variety of special equipment, but all gymnasts must have strength, poise and athletic skill.

Gymnastics in the Past

Gymnastics has been around for a very long time. Seven thousand years ago, female gymnasts performed routines for the Egyptian pharaohs. Through the ages, gymnasts have often earned a living by entertaining people. They were known as 'tumblers', and performed in travelling troupes or circuses.

Gymnastics has been a competitive sport for more than a hundred years. For example, there were gymnastics competitions at the first modern Olympics, which were held in 1896.

Modern Gymnastics

Today, most gymnasts train to take part in competitions. Elite gymnasts compete in events such as the Olympics Games, World Cups and World Championships.

Filip Ude of Croatia performs a floor exercise during an international artistic gymnastics competition in 2013.

Having a coach is vital for anyone who wants to improve their gymnastics. Coaches give advice on technique and fitness, as well as making sure that all the practices are done as safely as possible.

Types of Gymnastics

In competitions, gymnastics is divided into three separate categories: artistic gymnastics, rhythmic gymnastics and trampolining.

Artistic gymnastics is what most people think of when they hear someone talking about 'gymnastics'. Artistic gymnastics includes:

- For men: floor exercises, horizontal bar, parallel bars, pommel horse, rings and vault.
- For women: balance beam, floor exercises, uneven bars and vault.

This book is mostly about artistic gymnastics.

Judging and Scoring

Each time a gymnast completes a skill or routine in a competition, he or she is given a score.

Two groups of judges award two separate scores based on difficulty, and on how well the routine has been performed. These scores are then added together to give the final score. In the past it was possible to score a 'perfect' 10. Today credit is given for difficulty, so gymnasts often score more than 10.

Perfect 10

In 1976, Romanian gymnast Nadia Comaneci became the first to score a perfect 10 at the Olympic Games, on the uneven bars. She went on to score another six 10s at the Games.

Gymnastics Basics

At the gym there is a wide variety of apparatus. Each piece is used for different kinds of gymnastics. Apart from the apparatus, gymnasts do not need very much equipment. They use handguards and chalk to help them grip during some exercises, for example while swinging on the bars.

Clothing

Most beginner gymnasts wear shorts and gym vests. Once gymnasts become more experienced, female gymnasts usually wear leotards. Male gymnasts wear either shorts or longer trousers, plus gym vests. A tracksuit is also important for keeping warm between exercises. Some gymnasts wear shoes to protect their feet on the beam, but most perform in bare feet.

The Apparatus

There are eight major pieces of apparatus in a gymnastics competition. Some of these are used by both male and female gymnasts, others are used only by males, or only by females. There are six events for male gymnasts, and four for females. Most gymnasts enter every event, which gives them a chance to win an overall 'all-around' medal. But some specialists enter just one or two events, such as parallel bars or vault, and aim to win medals in those specific events.

These young gymnasts are wearing a mixture of clothing. The most important thing for beginners is that their clothes are not too loose, so they don't get in the way.

(From left to right) The balance beam, the pommel horse, the rings and the vaulting table are just a few of the pieces of apparatus used by gymnasts.

• Floor Area (males and females)

Gymnasts perform tumbling and balance skills (see pages 10–11). Females perform a routine to music that can last up to 90 seconds. Males perform for 70 seconds and without music.

• Horizontal Bar (males only)

The gymnast spins round and round the bar, sometimes letting go, changing his grip or twisting to add difficulty to the routine (see pages 16–17).

• Pommel Horse (males only)

The pommel horse has handles on top for the gymnast to hold on to. The gymnast performs routines based on swinging his body and legs around the horse (see pages 20–21).

• Rings (males only)

The gymnast hangs from the rings forming shapes, for example a cross-shape, with his body. During the routine he must try to keep the rings – which hang from cables – as still as possible (see pages 20–21).

• Parallel Bars (males only)

The gymnast performs handstands, swings, twists and other movements (see pages 18–19).

• Vaulting Area (males and females)

Male and female gymnasts run along a runway towards a springboard, which helps them leap up and over the vault table (see pages 12–13).

• Balance Beam (females only)

The gymnast performs balances, jumps, leaps and running steps along the 10cm-wide top of the beam (see pages 14–15).

• Uneven Bars (females only)

The gymnast performs similar skills to those done by men on the horizontal bar. There are two bars, so the routines can be very spectacular (see pages 16–17).

The Floor

Floor routines involve a combination of stunning tumbling sequences with skilful balances, twists and other manoeuvres.

The Floor Area

Floor routines are performed on a padded mat, inside an area measuring 12.2m square. Male and female gymnasts use the same size floor area. The padded area continues outside the square for safety, but if the gymnasts step or tumble outside the square accidentally, they lose points.

Handstand to High Forward Roll

1 First, the gymnast steps well forward to begin a handstand. From a strong starting position like this, she will be able to do a kick up that will leave her standing on her hands in balance.

2 Now the gymnast is in balance in the handstand: notice that her body and legs form a straight line. This is an ideal handstand: a curved back, or legs that do not stick straight up, will lose points.

3 Next the gymnast rolls her head forwards and lets her arms bend. Her legs stay straight up in the air, and she rolls downwards on a curved back.

Routines

The biggest feature of male gymnasts' floor routines is spectacular tumbling sequences, though other skills are also used. The routines have to show that the gymnast is flexible, strong and has good balance. He is expected to use each of the four corners of the floor at least once during the routine.

Unlike male floor exercises, female floor routines are set to vocal-free music. Their routines are choreographed, which means that they include some dance skills, as well as tumbles and balance skills.

Backflips can make up a spectacular part of floor routines – especially when peformed at speed.

Even just the edge of a heel touching the floor boundary will result in lost points if the judges spot it.

4 & 5 The gymnast bends her knees just as her bottom hits the floor, using the momentum of the roll to stand up.

6 The gymnast stands up straight, arms above her head and ready to perform the next skill. The best floor exercises link lots of different skills together smoothly.

Vaulting

Vaulting is one of the oldest gymnastics events. It has its roots in ancient Greece, where young men leapt over charging bulls to prove their bravery and agility.

Modern-day Vaulting

Despite the lack of charging bulls, modern-day vaulting still requires bravery. It can be dangerous, so it is vital to learn vaulting techniques only with a qualified coach.

The Handspring

Judging speed on the runway is an important part of vaulting. Not enough speed and the vault will be impossible to complete properly. Too much and it will be wild and uncontrolled.

1 Gymnasts keep the same long, slightly arched body shape all the way through a handspring. To do this, they need a reasonably fast run-up.

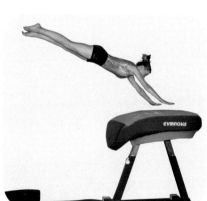

2 It is important to hit the springboard with speed, but also to be in control. Sprinting wildly in towards the board is dangerous.

3 As she leaps towards the vaulting table, the gymnast reaches up and forwards. It's important to keep looking ahead to where your hands will be placed.

4 Once her hands are firmly planted on the table, the thrust stage of the vault begins. The gymnast keeps her head still, and tightens her bottom muscles to help her legs come over.

The Stages of a Vault

Each vault is made up of seven crucial stages.

- The run-up.
- A hurdle step, which allows the vaulter to change from running to a two-footed landing on the springboard.
- The jump from the springboard.
- First flight, towards the vaulting table.
- The thrust, or pushing, stage, when the vaulter comes into contact with the vaulting table.
- Second flight, when the vaulter leaves the table.
- Landing, when vaulters bend their legs to absorb the force of the landing. They land flat on their feet, with their feet pointing slightly outwards.

The Handspring

This is one of the most commonly performed vaults, and also the one that is most often performed badly. Gymnasts can avoid developing bad habits by learning on a low-set vaulting table, increasing the height of the table only once their technique is perfect.

5 During the second flight stage of the vault, the gymnast aims to keeps her body in an arched shape and let her head drop back a little. This helps to keep enough rotation in the vault.

6 & 7 The gymnast must land with her feet together. As she lands the gymnast bends her knees to absorb the shock. Her arms are opened out to the side for balance. She then stands up straight, arms in the air, to finish the vault.

The Balance Beam

Only female gymnasts perform on the balance beam. It is the most difficult piece of apparatus and even a small mistake can – and often does – lead to a fall on to the padding beneath the beam.

Balance-beam Routines

Balance-beam routines are performed on a lightly padded strip of wood, 1.25m above the ground, 5m long, and just 10cm wide. Despite the beam being only just a little wider than most people's feet, top gymnasts perform leaps, twists and tumbling sequences along it.

Routines are divided into:

- A mount.
- A sequence of moves on the beam, which will include simple dance steps, leaps, rolls and jumps. Advanced gymnasts are even able to add some floor skills (such as backflips) to their beam routines.
- A dismount.

Forward Roll on the Beam

1 The gymnast starts in a balanced position, with one foot in front of the other.

2 From there, she crouches smoothly, keeping a straight back for good shape.

3 Rolling forwards, the gymnast grips the beam as she tucks her head into the roll and pushes off her front foot.

Learning Balance-beam Skills

To start with, beam skills are developed on the floor. Gymnasts begin by practising their skills on a line laid along the floor, or on a wide bench. Next they move to a low beam, before finally testing their skills on a real-life competition beam.

Pirouette Practice

To practise this move, put two pieces of masking tape on the floor 10cm apart. Pirouette on one foot 360 degrees (a full turn) between the pieces of tape.

4 If the roll has been straight and the gymnast has kept her feet together, her feet will hit the beam as she rolls forwards.

Simone Biles

United States of America
Date of birth: 14 March, 1997

Simone Biles began her senior career in 2011, and her performances are marked by great power and strength. She won gold at the US National Championships in 2013, 2014 and 2016. Having won a combined total of 19 Olympic and World Championship medals, she is the most decorated American gymnast.

All-around • Gold 2013, 2014 and 2015 World Championships, Gold 2016 Olympic Games
Team • Gold 2014 and 2015 World Championships, Gold 2016 Olympics
Floor exercise • Gold 2013, 2014 and 2015 World Championships, Gold 2016 Olympic Games
Balance beam • Gold 2014 and 2015 World Championships

5 The gymnast's arms are forward to help her continue the movement back to a standing position.

The Bars

Bar work is probably the most spectacular gymnastic event. The competitors show great bravery as they pick up speed by swinging round and round a thin bar, high in the air.

The Horizontal Bar

Men's bar work is done using a single bar. In competition, the bar is 2.75m above the ground, but most coaches start their students off on a bar about shoulder height. Each complete spin round the bar is called a giant. After building up speed with a succession of giants, advanced gymnasts let go of the bar and launch spectacular moves. They then either catch the bar and continue their routine, or dismount. There is always padding beneath the bar in case the gymnast falls.

A Swing

This young gymnast is training on just one of the uneven bars.

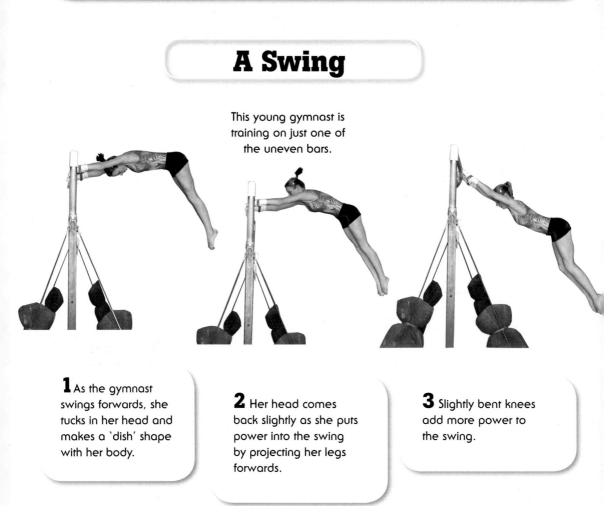

1 As the gymnast swings forwards, she tucks in her head and makes a 'dish' shape with her body.

2 Her head comes back slightly as she puts power into the swing by projecting her legs forwards.

3 Slightly bent knees add more power to the swing.

The Uneven Bars

Women compete on uneven or 'asymmetric' bars, one higher than the other. The bars are 2.46m and 1.66m above the ground. The gymnast swings round each bar, switching between the two in the blink of an eye.

Young female gymnasts train using just one of the asymmetric bars and move on to using both bars as they get stronger and more skilled.

Beth Tweddle

Great Britain
Date of birth: 1 April, 1985

Beth started gymnastics classes when she was seven years old and went on to become the most successful British gymnast ever. Her best event is the uneven bars, but she is an all-rounder, so much so that she won the title of British all-around Champion every year from 2001 to 2005. Beth is the first British gymnast to win medals on the world gymnastics stage, and the first ever to win an Olympic medal in individual women's gymnastics. Beth retired in 2013 on the anniversary of her Olympic Bronze medal win.

Uneven bars • Gold 2006, 2009, 2010 and 2011 European Championships • Gold 2006 and 2010 World Championships • Bronze 2012 Olympic Games
Floor exercise • Gold 2009 World Championships • Gold 2009 and 2010 European Championships

4 As the swing continues, the gymnast straightens her body.

5 At the end of the swing, her body is straight and her head tucked in.

17

The Parallel Bars

The parallel bars are used only by male gymnasts. The main skill on the bars is swinging, and the judges look for smooth swinging and flight of the body between moves.

The Equipment
Parallel bars are made up of two wooden or plastic bars 195cm above the ground, 350cm long and with a gap of 42–52cm between them. Underneath there is padding, in case the gymnast slips or falls.

The Swing
The swing is the crucial skill in parallel-bar work, and the first, most important thing young gymnasts learn. It works like a pendulum, with the gymnast's shoulders moving forwards as his feet go backwards. The swing begins from the shoulders and chest. The gymnast's body is held straight, but a slight kick of his feet at the end of the forward swing helps keep the swing going.

The Upstart on Parallel Bars

1 The gymnast swings forwards on the bars, feet out in front.

2 Hanging on with his hands, the gymnast lets his body extend out as it swings forwards.

The swing can be done while the gymnast is resting on his hands, from a hanging position, and from an upper-arm position.

The Upstart

This allows a gymnast to get into a raised position on the bars, resting on his hands. The upwards thrust happens during the second part of the movement, and has to be timed carefully with the pendulum movement of the gymnast's swing.

The Routine

A typical routine on the bars usually includes:

• Swinging skills.

• Flips and turns, where the gymnast changes direction or spins around.

• Strength positions, where the gymnast holds a difficult shape without moving.

• A dismount, in which the gymnast swings off the bars and finishes the routine standing beside them.

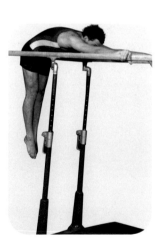

3 A quick bend at the hips brings the gymnast's legs up close to his face.

4 As the gymnast begins to swing back, his legs come away to an angle of about 70–80 degrees from his body.

5 As the gymnast's shoulders rise up on the return swing, he extends his hips and pushes downwards on to the bars with straight arms. The gymnast's body is now raised above the bars, and he is able to rest on his hands.

19

The Pommel Horse and Rings

As with the parallel bars, only male gymnasts compete on the pommel horse and rings. Both these pieces of apparatus require a combination of technique and strength.

The Pommel Horse

On the pommel horse, gymnasts swing their legs round and round the horse, supporting themselves with their hands on the 'pommels' – the hand holds – and on the top of the horse itself.

As they swing round, they perform a series of manoeuvres with their legs, including:

- Double leg circles, where the gymnast's legs are held together as he pivots round and round on the pommels.
- Flares, where the gymnast's outside leg is pointed straight into the air as his lower leg passes the pommel.
- Scissors, where the gymnast pivots to and fro on the pommel, lifting and dropping his legs on either side of the horse in a scissors movement.
- A handstand leading to dismount.

The Rings

On the rings, gymnasts perform a combination of swings and strength moves. Strength moves are motionless positions that require good balance and control of the rings. One of the most famous is the crucifix, where the gymnast holds his arms straight out to the sides and hangs still, with legs together pointing straight downwards.

A Smooth Swing

A smooth swing is crucial for the rings. Without it, it will be impossible to stop the rings swaying. Keeping downward pressure on the rings all the time helps to keep the swing smooth.

British gymnast Max Whitlock performs an exercise on the pommel horse at the European Championships in 2013.

Swinging on the Rings

1 The gymnast swings forwards with arms and legs fully extended.

2 As the gymnast's weight comes forward, he tenses his body and legs from the hips, and keeps downward force on the rings. This tensing adds momentum to the swing.

3 The gymnast comes towards the top of the swing. He keeps tension on the rings, which have moved outwards slightly as his body rose up.

4 As the gymnast comes through the top of his swing, he relaxes his body.

5 The gymnast swings down and back towards his starting position, ready for another smooth swing.

Rhythmic Gymnastics

Rhythmic gymnastics is mainly for female gymnasts, although it is increasingly popular with male gymnasts in a few countries, especially in Asia. It combines gymnastic and dance skills.

Equipment

In rhythmic gymnastics, competitors use additional pieces of equipment as part of their routine. These are:

- A rubber or plastic ball, about 20cm across.
- Clubs, which look similar to jugglers' clubs.
- A wooden or plastic hoop, about 85cm across.
- A long ribbon on the end of a short stick.
- A rope with a knot at each end.

Building a Routine

Only one piece of equipment is used in each routine. The equipment is a crucial part of the combination of dance and gymnastics skills.

Types of Contest

There are different types of contest for rhythmic gymnastics:

- In individual contests, the gymnasts must use four of the five pieces of equipment.
- In team contests, members of five-person teams split the five pieces of equipment between them.

The Italian team perform a routine with balls and ribbons at the Rhythmic Gymnastics World Championships in 2013.

Russian rhythmic gymnast Yana Kudryavtseva performs with the hoop at a competition in 2015. She was the all-around World Champion in 2013 and 2014.

Rhythmic gymnastics was first included in the World Gymnastics Championships in 1963. The sport has been part of the Olympic Games since the 1984 Los Angeles Olympics.

Scoring

Each routine is given a score of up to 20 points. The score is based on two elements of the gymnast's routine:

- Technical difficulty.
- How well the skills have been done.

The aim of this scoring system is to reward gymnasts with good technical skills.

Men's Rhythmic Gymnastics

Men's rhythmic gymnastics is particularly popular in Asia, especially in Japan. There, the sport combines rhythmic gymnastics, artistic gymnastics and wushu martial arts. No ball is used, and routines include tumbling.

Equipment

Ribbon
The ribbon is long and light, and can be thrown or waved to make designs in the air around the gymnast. The designs include snakes, spirals and loops.

Hoop
The hoop creates a space for the gymnast to use. Her routine includes movements through the hoop – for example, forward rolls.

Ball
Routines using a ball combine spectacular throws and catches with gymnastic movements.

Rope
The rope can be held taut or loose, in one hand or two. It winds and unwinds around the gymnast like a serpent.

Clubs
Gymnasts use the clubs for asymmetric movements, rolling, twisting, throwing and catching them first with one arm then the other.

Trampolining

Anyone who has tried trampolining in a friend's garden knows what fun it can be. Trampolining is part of the world of gymnastics.

The First Trampolines

A man called George Nissen made the first trampolines in the 1930s. He based his invention on the safety nets used by circus trapeze artists. The principles of the trampoline have been the same ever since: a flexible, bouncy mat with springs around the edges, which allows you to bounce up and down to a great height.

Modern Equipment

Modern competition trampolines measure 4.3m by 2.1m. Around the edges of the trampoline are thick, padded mats called safety platforms. A cross marks the centre of the trampoline. Trampolinists aim to land as near as possible to this cross for each bounce. Too far away, and they will lose points from their score.

Safe Training

During training, trampolinists sometimes wear a spotting belt. This is a belt that is attached to overhead pulleys. It allows the coach to stop the trampolinist falling dangerously.

The different landing positions used in trampolining: (top left) landing 'to feet'; (bottom left) landing 'to seat', in a sitting-down position with the legs straight ahead; (top right) landing 'to front', with the hands under the chin; (bottom right) landing 'to back', on your back with arms and legs pointing upwards.

Trampoline Pioneer

Ted Blake was a British trampoline pioneer who introduced trampolining into Europe. In 1964, he organised the first trampoline World Championships in London.

The three basic body shapes used during a trampolining routine: (top left) the tuck; (above) the pike; and (left) straight.

Competitions

In 2000, trampolining became one of the Olympic gymnastics disciplines. During their routines, trampolinists perform a series of skills including single, double or even triple somersaults and twists. They must start and finish each routine on their feet, and aim to hold their body shape throughout each skill. There are two types of competition: individual and synchronised.

Individual Contests

Trampolinists perform two routines, each with 10 skills. In the compulsory routine, four of the skills are required by the regulations. The trampolinist chooses the other six. In the voluntary routine, the trampolinist gets to choose all 10 skills.

Synchronised Contests

In synchronised contests, two trampolinists on side-by-side trampolines perform the exact same routine. They aim to stay in perfect time with each other, with each looking like a mirror image of the other.

Competitions

Gymnastics competitions are run at every level, from local club championships to the Olympics and World Championships. Whatever the event, every gymnast aims to improve his or her personal best score.

Olympics and World Championships

The Olympics and World Championships are the toughest competitions in the world of gymnastics. The Olympics, which only takes place every four years, is the one every gymnast dreams of winning.

The gymnasts at the Olympics and World Championships are entered as national teams of six. The competition is divided into four parts: team qualifying, team finals, all-around finals and event finals:

Young gymnasts take part in local competitions.

Team managers and coaches help the gymnasts, making sure they are ready for their events.

- Team qualifying: up to five of the six gymnasts in each team compete on each apparatus. The best four of their scores are counted towards the team total. (This is called the '6–5–4 format'.)

- Team finals: the top eight teams from the qualifying session compete, but this time only three of the six gymnasts can compete on each piece of apparatus. All three scores count.

- All-around finals: the top 24 gymnasts from the team qualifying session qualify for the all-around finals. Only two gymnasts per country are allowed.

- Event finals: these are competitions for the top eight gymnasts for each piece of apparatus. Only two gymnasts from each country can qualify for each apparatus.

The World Cup and Other Competitions

The World Cup is a series of major gymnastics competitions that takes place around the world every year. These and other competitions do not always work in the same way as the Olympics. In the World Cup, for example, there are no team competitions at all. Only individual all-around and apparatus contests take place.

Kōhei Uchimura

Japan
Date of birth: 3 January, 1989

Uchimura began gymnastics at the age of three, and joined Japan's national team in 2007. He is famous for winning six consecutive World Championship all-around golds (from 2009 to 2015), and the Olympic all-around title in 2012 and 2016. He is known for his difficult and accurate routines, and many people consider him to be the greatest male gymnast of all time.

All-around • Gold 2009, 2010, 2011, 2013, 2014, 2015 World Championships • Gold 2012, 2016 Olympic Games
Floor exercise • Gold 2011 World Championships
Parallel bars • Gold 2013 World Championships

27

Record Holders

Most Men's Olympic Titles
• The men's team all-around title has been won seven times by Japan (1960, 1964, 1968, 1972, 1976, 2004 and 2016).

• Two gymnasts have won six men's individual gold medals, the biggest number ever:
Boris Shakhlin (USSR) won one in 1956, four (two shared) in 1960, and one in 1964;
Nikolay Andrianov (USSR) won one in 1972, four in 1976, and one in 1980.

Most Men's Olympic Medals
• Nikolay Andrianov (USSR) won a record 15 Olympic medals (seven gold, five silver, and three bronze) from 1972 to 1980.

• Aleksandr Dityatin (USSR) won a record eight medals at one Olympic Games, in Moscow, Russia (then USSR), in 1980. He won three gold, four silver and one bronze.

Most Women's Olympic Medals
• Larisa Latynina (USSR) won six individual gold medals and three team golds from 1956 to 1964. She also won five silver and four bronze medals, making an Olympic-record total of 18.

Most Women's Olympic Titles
• The USSR won the Olympic women's title a record 10 times (from 1952 to 1980, and in 1988 and 1992). The last title was won by a Unified Team from the republics of the former USSR.

• Vera Čáslavská-Odložil (Czech Republic) holds the record for the most individual gold medals: three in 1964 and four (one shared) in 1968.

Most World and Olympic titles
• Kōhei Uchimura (Japan) won ten World Championships titles between 2009 and 2015; six consecutive all-around golds 2009 – 2015 as well as golds in the floor exercise in 2011, the parallel bars in 2013 and horozontal bar in 2015. In 2012 and 2016 he won the all-around gold medal at the Olympic Games.

Glossary

All-around Performing and competing on all of the different pieces of gymnastics apparatus. To win an all-around medal women gymnasts must compete in four events, and male gymnasts in six.

Apparatus A piece of equipment designed for a special purpose. In gymnastics, competitions take place on one of seven possible pieces of apparatus: floor, vaulting table, rings, pommel horse, parallel bars, asymmetric bars and beam.

Asymmetric Not equal or the same on both sides. In the asymmetric bars, for example, one bar is higher than the other.

Average The middle of a group of scores or numbers. One way of finding an average is to add up all the scores, then divide them by the number of scores. So, for example, if three judges score a gymnast 7.85, 8.20 and 8.35, the average would be (7.85 + 8.20 + 8.35) ÷ 3, which is 8.13.

Choreograph To put together a sequence of steps and moves to create a performance.

Czechoslovakia Former country in central Europe, which divided into the Czech Republic and the Slovak Republic on 1 January 1993.

Dismount In gymnastics, the process of getting off a piece of apparatus such as a pommel horse to end the routine.

Flight Movement through the air.

Martial arts Styles of fighting, for example taekwondo or judo.

Momentum Forwards movement, especially at an increasing speed.

Paralysis Not being able to move. In humans, paralysis is usually caused by damage to the spine.

Pharaohs The rulers of ancient Egypt.

Pirouette To spin on one foot.

Pommel The curved handle that is attached at both ends to the top of a pommel horse.

Rotation A turning or spinning motion.

Specialists In gymnastics, specialists are people who usually compete on a particular piece of apparatus.

Trapeze A horizontal bar attached at each end to a rope. In circuses, gymnastic tricks by people swinging from the trapeze are always a popular attraction.

Troupes Groups of performers.

USSR Short for the Union of Soviet Socialist Republics, a country that existed from 1922 to 1991. It then split into many new countries, of which the largest and most powerful is Russia.

Vocal Using the voice, especially for singing.

Wushu Chinese martial arts.

Websites

www.british-gymnastics.org
The home website of British Gymnastics, with news about the British team, latest competitions, results, information about technique and coaching, and help in finding a gymnastics club near you.

www.olympic.org
The official website of the Olympic Movement, with a section that deals with gymnastics. There are profiles of famous Olympic gymnasts, as well as information about the different gymnastics disciplines.

www.fig-gymnastics.org
The home site of the FIG (the Fédération Internationale de Gymnastique), the world governing body for gymnastics, this is the place to find out about rules, clothing and results from world events.

http://www.bbc.co.uk/sport/gymnastics
News from the world of gymnastics on the BBC website.

Note to parents and teachers: every effort has been made by the Publishers to ensure that these websites are suitable for children, that they are of the highest educational value, and that they contain no inappropriate or offensive material. However, because of the nature of the Internet, it is impossible to guarantee that the contents of these sites will not be altered. We strongly advise that Internet access is supervised by a responsible adult.

Index